sad boy /
detective

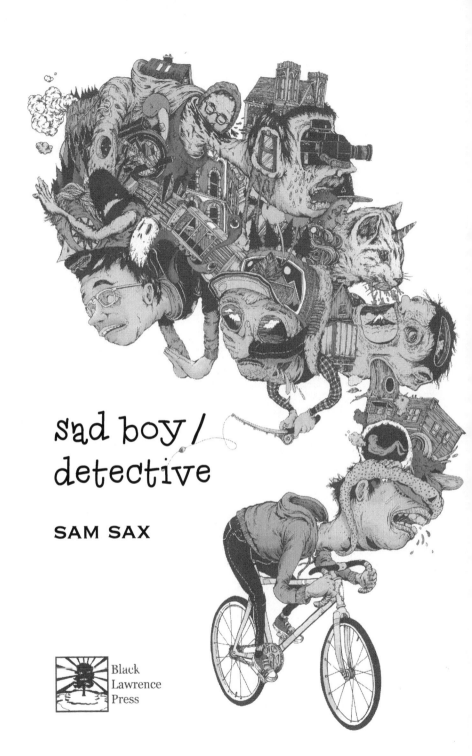

sad boy /
detective

SAM SAX

Black
Lawrence
Press

Black
Lawrence
Press

www.blacklawrence.com

Executive Editor: Diane Goettel
Chapbook Editor: Kit Frick
Book and cover design: Amy Freels
Cover art: *Nerd Herder* by Pat Perry. Used with permission.

Published 2015 by Black Lawrence Press.
Printed in the United States.

for my family

There is nothing more thrilling in this world, I think, than having a child that is yours and yet is mysteriously a stranger.

—**Agatha Christie**

פֿאַר װײבער און פֿאַר מאַנסבילן װאָס זײַנען אַזוי װי װײבער, דאָס הייסט זיי קענען ניט לערנען

Contents

the boy detective gets his start

birth is a trauma he never expected to survive.
some time, twelve years deep, the amniotic fluid dried
and he became a boy. looked in a clean mirror, saw
mystery. from then on the boy dealt only in ciphers.
the year he stopped swaddling himself in deep red
sheets, we knew he was bound for something unsolvable.
the year he broke a florescent bulb in his father's study
to watch a flame spill across all those old books.
what safe horror, to skin a beam of light and only find
more light. to break free of your mother into a world
so bright it's impossible to understand. when even language
is a photocopy of someone else's speaking mouth.
it didn't make sense: slim key in a galaxy of holes.
no.   he had to figure it out.

the boy detective discovers his parents having sex

take a sound. stretch it into the most horrible
shape you can imagine. the boy was curious.
was it the house that moaned like that, caught
in some muted storm? if you stare at a door
long enough, you can see through it. placed
his eye to the key hole and his whole body went
stiff when faced with his origin. empty square
of a cowboy gripping the pale horse by its
knotted mane. her giant head lifted a foot
from the bed, reigns flexed in his hands. heard
her whimper with the light switch. the pastoral
picture of a mare painted over a far more hideous
image. he still remembers the sound, loving the steel
bit in her mouth, a door hinge squealing open.

the boy detective burns ants

it began with awe ballooning
in his stomach. an insect that moves
only when his brothers do. holds
itself over a hundred times to keep
his family alive. the boy detective's
mother even smells sad. no matter
what strange thing he brings in from
outside. her mouth lays flat as a dead
animal, tells him into the sun, into
the bright march forward with all
you can carry. he redirects god, smoke
rises in tiny screams. insect meat
cooking inside its shining exoskeleton.
their mouths don't open once.

the boy detective investigates death

from the hallway you can hear the machines bleat
their pastiche chorus. one body leaving the world,
another screaming out into its empty place. the boy
sits on the edge of an empty hospital bed. it has been
made to look neat, as if his mother could be folded
and bleached out. but he knows how to listen close,
to feel the weight left behind inside the mattress.
he wonders if he can calculate the precise mass
of a soul this way. what matter is left behind
by the dying? he places a stethoscope to the hospital
sheets, listens for evidence this place is the weigh
station between asylums he suspects.
in the silence he decides that each time he lies down
he dies, and each time he rises up   he is born again.

the boy detective discovers his body

he knows when the lights in his room black out
his body can become whatever he imagines.
some nights a dragon. some nights a field of wet
thumbs. on the best nights he is still a boy
with clothing that burns from his skin until
it's just him floating a full foot off the bed naked
and trying to open himself so light will pour
out into the blackness. the first time he came
the room exploded into a clean bright bandage,
every question raging through his blood dulled.
his own private analgesic. the knowledge that
no matter what matter spills out of him it will
always be light. the perfect hypothesis.
the bed that swallows him when he is done.

the boy detective home from (beauty) school

he was forced into manicuring the strange
landscapes of his body. the sun yellow bus was full
of two-fisted laughing children. he'd pick a window
seat and watch the lawns and gardens spin clean
past him, all cared for by good men. the seats
behind were teaming with green insects teething
at his neck, pulling the hairs out by the root.
they laughed at the places his body bulged
or did not. the brambled foliage on his upper lip,
the dirt beneath his nails. one girl gripped tweezers
like a pair of metal mandibles. removed the locks
that grew between his eyes. the bus leaves him
sheared on his front steps. he finds the nearest dirty
mirror, digs a wet hole. plants himself there.

the boy detective and his father visit the video store

the boy wanders the videotape canyons. he only
has eyes for one story. anywhere a boy can stay
a boy. *pan* in his various incarnations: in french,
in hook, in cartoon, in music. his father only
has eyes for horror. somewhere a girl can be stripped
of her skin and the world goes on turning. somewhere
rusted nails shoot up from the scalp and the creature
grows more teeth when dragged into the light.
they spend hours combing the store. the boy lost
in one aisle or another. father fingering the box
they'll go watch, one where no one gets out alive.
sitting in the dark, the boy looks at the shadow
beside him. hums the song in his head. *never gonna be
a man. i wont. like to see somebody try and make me.*

the boy detective's wet dream

he's snapped awake and he's drowning.
the boy left behind, a vulgar warmth
gathered around his sex, an unwelcome
wetness he prays is urine.
what would happen if instead of growing
cold the lake he made—burned? if the lake
became a river he could cross out
of humiliation into eternity.
the new burden of his comforter, cement
hardening into the statue of a winged child
between his legs, his shame born less out
of hunger than his body's refusal to be trained.
he brings one finger to his lips and tastes
gasoline. he cleans himself in the dark.

the boys detective tries his first pair of glasses

the world didn't get any clearer.
everything behind the sheets of glass
just grew sharper edges. he could see
in the dark. his eyes,   windows
glowing in an abandoned dormitory.
the smeared features of his classmates
narrowed into yard sticks, the blackboard
got gaunt, the backs of boys' heads
formed black tentacles, their eyes buckshot.
so he took his eyes out. left them on the dresser
until each room became a blur of color again,
magic-marker drawn map wilting in the rain.
a world where each new scowling face
doesn't tell its story quite so plainly.

the boy detective in the big game

he braids grass in the outfield. flat green strands
of hair. the earth, a woman's skull in need of caring,
he cares for her. hospice outside the diamond.
grecian, double, french, reverse. runs his hands
through the dirt and feels her release beneath him.
takes off his metal cleats to a sigh. the boys know
when the ball's hit left center everyone's going home.
if only coach took him off the field in his arms,
let him make the calls, or held him under water.
black paint on the cheekbones, hands huge
and leather, eyes narrowed into a chain link fence.
if only the boy were born an olympian or man
or better kind of boy. at home he grips his bat
with both hands, swings until the lights black out.

the boy detective searches for love

if you look hard enough into another person
you see yourself. that's how the boy first found
love. the mirror's veil falling in the eyes of another
boy across the cafeteria counter.
everyone else was white noise as they both ate
white bread sandwiches in silence. their sneakers
touched beneath the table, quiet current passed
through their rubber soles and spread open eyes.
later the boy detective took him into his mouth.
noted the sponged expansion of blood. conjectured
this boy would buck when he ran his tongue over
the frenulum. and he did. gunned down deer,
twitching between life and its opposite. love
is spilt milk. is control, anyway that you can.

the boy detective dresses up as a girl detective

late in october the leaves take off their green
costumes, fall about themselves until they crunch
below your feet. halloween is a night when people
dress up exactly as they are. the hormonal
neighborhood boys with ski-masks and eggs.
the empty women brimming over with wine glasses.
the detective only puts on a mouthful of rouge,
a gold dragonfly brooch. she walks into the night
by herself. goes door to door. grown folks open
for her. ask what she's dressed as. she says myself.
bats her vampire eyelashes, sashays down the street
flooded with dead men and memories. no one looks
how they should. halloween stretches into spring,
she stays painted long after everyone gets undressed.

the boy detective waits up for his brother

thirteen years of waiting for a door that never swings
open. each time the wind picks up some trash and drops
it sounds like a footstep. on the front porch with older
boys, smoke hanging between their fingers.
he smells bourbon through the door. fully dressed
under his blanket for the night his brother decides to come
back and teach him to drink. he's been practicing
for that moment so the boys won't laugh when his throat
rejects the liquor. he's taught himself to enjoy
the taste of poison. to turn his gag reflex into a precise
instrument, laughing alone in his father's chair. glass
tumbler dimming the room in his hand.
he never had a brother. not really. just some wind, just
some light casting shadows in the shape of an older boy.

the boy detective does research at the public library

this place used to be for learning. now it's where dead
things go to live: mausoleum, museum, photograph,
pen. the books are still and breathing, their perfect
bound spines on display, flaunting bar codes.
let me open for you, they say. this place and the books
inside are one mystery that unlocks into another.
he unlatches the bathroom door, finds a man trembling
on the tile floor. metal pen needled into his blood.
the boy forgets why he came. wishes people were marked
into easier categories. where you could read their dust
jacket before asking the man if he was okay or lifting
his wet face from the white floor. before
staring into the bottomless nothing of his mouth,
losing yourself there, never climbing out.

the boy detective loses love

there should be a word for how the world turns
to amber resin with a long dead wasp gasping
inside when somebody leaves you. the boy tries
to catalogue each betrayal, rage shouting
up through his skin. this way he could understand.
marker on the wall, lipstick on the mirror, ink
spreading its arms across every page in his notebook.
each letter becomes a name, each name a shadow
walking away. this is stasis. this is a fish split
open and thrashing on a dock beneath a sky
with no stars. this is how all the light gets
swallowed. how we store our sorrow in clear
glass jars that tint the winter's light and keep
us warm through the coldest months.

the boy detective is punished

we are long past the days of the switch.
the detective was thankful and heartbroken
about this, wrist ground to nub chalk dust
against blackboard. *speak up* written until
the words broke into letters, the letters into shapes,
the shapes into a train with wheels bolted on and
screaming. he dreams of being sent into the world
to choose the thickness of his punishment.
to balance how much pain is deserved for what's
inside him. to be bent over a wood desk and beaten
by something so like his own hands. but this iron
horse chalk ride is a different kind of discipline.
it strips his wrist down to the bone like an oak limb.
it teaches him the lesson. it's written in him now.

the boy detective analyzes his hands

enough nails for a chair and two christs,
knuckles white as a burning filament, palms
soft-boiled fruit. this boy's never known labor,
except one kind. he can fit three fingers
inside himself without crying. four if he's been
drinking spirits. he knows how to lift
and to spread. how the human fist evolved
through violence. how the softest
still hold their own brutality. strange,
how different the hand looks wrapped
around a throat than a pen. becomes
almost an entirely different appendage.
blood carries red ink into the fingers,
it stains everything you touch.

the boy detective digs his cat's grave

he opens the earth. she was the worst cat
in the world. remarkable only in her cruelty
and then it was the cruelty of all cats, so
unremarkable. he hated her for that and even
his hatred was plain. he tries to remember
she was a living thing pulled from another
thing that lived. no hope of children. this
should make him sad. but his teeth flash
halogen and drunk as he digs the tiny grave,
as he stitches the cat's limbs, carves another
eye, wraps its mangled body in construction
paper. years from now,
another boy will find this museum curio,
digging for answers in the earth.

the boy detective visits a palm reader

she handed him a card with a moon, two stars,
a candle, and an old man on it. it read, *i can lift
you out of sorrow and darkness*, so of course he went.
climbed the victorian steps, split the cloth door
with his hand how an oar parts black water,
crept inside. she was seated at a wood desk floating
a full foot off the dark blue floor. when he sat, he swore
the table bobbed up and down above the carpet.
she asked for his hand, laid it down like a cracked
mast, the sail spread out over the waves. her dark
eyes sank back into her skull as she charted him
by his stars. the life-line that capsized and anchored.
the candle that shined from the lighthouse. the old
man, moon white and silent below the water.

the boy detective gets scared straight

men in their night blue button-up uniforms
take the children through the theater of incarceration.
the locked-in leather backseat of the squad car,
what steel feels like against the wrist. at the station
the children leave their fingerprints and take ink
into general population. the bars aren't the kind
you'll find on television, here everything is glass.
men in tan jumpsuits are brought in to scare
the children into children. they yell from their deepest
register, tell what kinds of breakage happen in the skin
and the brain. the boy imagines spending his life
this way. to have a man stand above him,
tell him what he is. to be taken up in arms,
how nice that would be, to be given a uniform.

the boy detective meets the man of his dreams

in the alley behind the eagle, men change into their true
shape. the boy sits between two trash tins and watches
snakes swallow. every time the door unbolts, black light
pours and a figure steps out to meet himself. tonight, the man
sprouts six arms, passes a cigarette between all of them.
fat lipped as if he'd been slugged in the face and the swelling
forgot itself. he stands there, smoking, stares right at the boy
who does his best to blend into garbage. becomes a rat
in the half light. with six hands the man points to a car door.
the two climb in and the boy learns to unhinge his jaw, to claw
at the edges of his body until the terrarium glass fogs over
in one hot breath. passersby hear the moans of a child being
torn from the light. inside the dark car he watches the man
transform. a father, an electrical storm, a bird of prayer.

the boy detective gets detected

it wasn't ugly until someone saw him do it.
simple investigation of the body and its limits.
what could be more natural then wanting to find
what's under your skin? how do you know
for sure it's just bone and muscle in there? the boy
had to find out. he'd always suspected an old map
wrapped up in the cartilage, a drunk compass spinning
toward a place with more mystery. which brought
him to this school bathroom once a week. between
anatomy and the end of the day. to split a new section
of wrist open hoping to find more than just blood.
but today, a pair of eyes thrust themselves through
the stall divider. saw the detective hard and naked
and hardly moving. pen jabbed into his forearm,

his findings, exactly as he'd predicted.

the boy detective is dead

and nobody really understands. you can tell
how the eulogies all say he was *inquisitive* and
interested. an eye for mystery with a future
that could have been *anything* or *important*.
they don't understand. what the boy saw move
inside his gnarled hand, up through the open cunt
of his left arm. what black teeth winked at him.
what radiator whispered, *closer to the dark*.
the doctors and professional feelers didn't know
what to do. or why the magnifying glass had turned
inward and the same word kept appearing in his
tiny spiral notebook. the ink's hatred of the word.
the most powerful thing in the world contained
inside its ugly body. the light when it is cut out.

Acknowledgments

BORDERLANDS:
>   the boy detective gets his start
>   the boy detective waits up for his brother

NAILED:
>   the boy detective discovers his parents having sex
>   the boy detective searches for love
>   the boy detective investigates death
>   the boy detective burns ants
>   the boy detective loses love

TUPELO QUARTERLY:
>   the boy detective's wet dream
>   the boy detective is punished (*as* the boy
>   detective undergoes corporeal punishment)

Thanks to Hieu Minh Nguyen, Cameron Awkward-Rich,
Danez Smith, Tatyana Brown, Nic Alea, The New Sh!t Show,
my family, & heartbreak. Without whom these poems wouldn't
be possible.

Photo: Chris Unguez

sam sax is a 2015 NEA Creative Writing Fellow and Poetry Fellow at The Michener Center for Writers where he serves as the Editor-in-chief of *Bat City Review*. He's the two-time Bay Area Grand Slam Champion & author of the chapbooks *A Guide to Undressing Your Monsters* (Button 2014), *sad boy / detective* (Black Lawrence 2015), *All The Rage* (Sibling Rivalry 2016), & is co-editor of the anthology *The Dead Animal Handbook* (University of Hell 2016). His poems are forthcoming in *The Beloit Poetry Journal*, *Boston Review*, *Indiana Review*, *Ninth Letter*, *Poetry Magazine*, *Pleiades*, *TriQuarterly* + other journals.